war natürlich der Steuereinnehmer! Er stand am Laden-
tisch, vom Schein der roten Glaskugel beleuchtet, und sagte
gerade; »Ich möchte ein Lot Vitriol.«

»Justin«, rief der Apotheker, »bring mal das Acidum sul-
furicum her!«

Dann wandte er sich an Emma, die nach Madame Homais'
Zimmer hinaufgehen wollte:

»Nein, bleiben Sie nur hier, es lohnt nicht, sie kommt
gleich herunter. Wärmen Sie sich inzwischen am Ofen ...
Entschuldigen Sie bitte ... Guten Tag, Doktor! (denn der
Apotheker pflegte sich dieses Titels mit Vorliebe zu bedie-
nen, als ob etwas von seinem Glanze auf ihn selbst ein paar
Strahlen werfe) ... Aber nimm dich in acht und wirf mir
die Mörser nicht um! Und dann holst du ein paar Stühle
aus dem kleinen Zimmer! Du weißt ganz genau, daß die
Fauteuils im Salon geschont werden sollen.«

Und Homais stürzte aus dem Zimmer, um selbst nach sei-
nen Sesseln zu sehen, aber Binet verlangte noch ein Lot
Zuckersäure.

»Zuckersäure?« fragte der Apotheker verächtlich. »Kenne
ich nicht! Gibt es nicht! Sie wollen wahrscheinlich Oxalsäure? Also Oxalsäure, nicht wahr?«

Binet setzte ihm auseinander, daß er ein bißchen davon
brauche, um sich ein selbsterfundenes Putzmittel für sein
verrostetes Jagdgerät zu bereiten. Emma zitterte. Der Apotheker meinte: »Gewiß; das Wetter ist ungünstig, der Feuch-

»Sie hätten schon von weitem rufen müssen!« schrie er,
bemerkbar machen!«

»Wenn man ein Gewehr sieht, muß man sich immer gleich
Der Steuereinnehmer suchte dadurch seine eigene Angst
zu bemänteln; denn da eine Verordnung des Präfekten be-
stand, nach der die Jagd auf Wildenten nur vom Kahn aus
betrieben werden durfte, machte Binet sich trotz seiner Ach-
tung vor den Gesetzen einer Übertretung schuldig. Deshalb
glaubte er, jede Minute einer Feldhüter kommen zu hören,
Doch diese Aufregung erhöhte sein Vergnügen, und wenn
er allein in seiner Tonne saß, war er stolz auf sein Jagd-
glück und seine Schlauheit.

Als er Emma erkannte, fiel ihm ein großer Stein vom Her-
zen, und er begann sofort eine Unterhaltung mit ihr.

»Es ist nicht gerade, die Kälte prickelt!« Sie sind heute schon
recht früh aus. Er fuhr fort: »Sie sind heute schon
bei der Amme, wo mein Kind
nicht! Er fuhr fort: schon seit Morgen-
....inen?« man auch

Contributors

Francesca Maria
Junis Sultan
Jenna Greene
Becky Parker Geist
Edward Willett
Indar Maharaj
Roger Leslie
Benedict Stuart
J L Hill
David Godolphin
J. J. Fauser
PD Alleva
Michelle Swann
A.A. Hadi White
Randy Miller
Dr Frank L Douglas
Val D. Greenwood
June Gillam
Cheryl Bond-Nelms
Barbara Galutia Regis M S Pa-C
Jeff Meyer

Review Tales
A Book Magazine For Indie Authors

Founder & Editor in Chief: S. Jeyran Main
Publisher: Review Tales Publishing & Editing Services
Print & Distribution: IngramSparks
Cover Photo: Pexels moldy vintages
ISBN 978-1-988680-32-3 (Paperback)
ISBN 978-1-988680-33-0 (Digital)
www.jeyranmain.com
For all inquiries, please get in touch with us directly.

Special thanks to:
Scott Hughes
Onlinebookclub.org

Dedicated to Babak Babi

Table of Contents

Editor's Notes

Summer always becomes the time when we vacate, and what better way to do so than with this year's summer edition? We get to interview Dr Roger Leslie and have him talk about his experience as a writer and how he focuses and prioritises to ensure he allocates the right time for writing. Francesca Maria writes horror fiction and combats her fears by playing characters in haunted places. We also learn how memoirs can be used to heal the writer and give back to the readers.

While we take the time to read the seventh edition, I would like to let everyone know that this magazine would not have been able to become close to what it is if it was not for the love and support of the authors who feature, purchase and socially share it.

True, we do live in the days and age where everything is digitalized, but at least there is hope as we have kept the love for reading printed books and magazines.

Here goes to many more editions! Let's have fun this summer because we all need it.

Founder & Editor-in-chief
Review Tales Magazine - Publishing & Editing Services

Author Confessions

Write What Scares You
by Francesca Maria

As a horror writer, I shine a light into dark places. I hunt for the creepy, the crawly, the insidious and all things that hide in shadows and go bump in the night. And let me share a little secret—I'm afraid of the dark, always have been, ever since I was a little girl growing up in a haunted house.

I'm afraid of the crack left open between closet doors. I'm afraid of the sounds left by a house settling. I'm afraid of hidden things that can spring out at any time. I'm afraid of a lot of things.

So, to combat my fears, I pick up a pen and write. I place my characters in haunted places, where evil lurks behind every creaky door. I write about the real horrors of death, grief, losing control and powerlessness.

I write what scares me as a way of exorcising these demons. By bringing fears out of the shadows and onto the page, they no longer have the same visceral hold. Writing gives me the power to control the narrative: what happens to whom, when, why and how.

I wrote my first short story at age six. It was about a group of kids that stumbled onto a haunted house at the end of their cul-de-sac.

The kids find and conquer a monster lurking under the house. That was my way of dealing with the real-life horror of living in a haunted house. I placed kids my age in a similar setting but gave them an ending where they were victorious, defeating the thing that scared them. It was empowering.

In the early days of the pandemic, I was gripped with debilitating fear. So, like my six-year-old self, I started writing. My short story collection, <u>They Hide: Short Stories to Tell in the Dark</u>, emerged from that. In the collection, I tackled the themes I struggled with during Covid: lack of control, powerlessness, anxiety and loss. Writing helped to bring me out of my panic attacks and gave me back a sense of control.

Francesca Maria is an award-winning, bestselling dark fiction author. They Hide: Short Stories to Tell in the Dark from Brigids Gate Press debuted at #1 in Amazon's Horror Short Stories. She is also the creator of the Black Cat Chronicles comic book series. Her fiction and essays are found in Crystal Lake Publishing's Shallow Waters series and anthologies, Death's Garden Revisited, and the upcoming Under the Stairs anthology. You can find her at <u>francescamaria.com</u>.

Growing with New Challenges by Junis Sultan

It was quite a journey until my book BROTHERS AND STRANGERS: A GERMAN-IRAQI MEMOIR got published. In 2011 I realized how broken I was from the yearlong repercussions of the Gulf War, our flight to Germany, and ethnic and religious conflicts in my family and our new environment.

I wanted to understand what happened, heal and not just survive, and give back something good to others. That's why I began writing this memoir. I have kept a journal since I was 15 years old, so writing has always been my way to process things and find meaning. Still, it took me some years to finish this memoir as I faced some challenges: dealing with re-traumatization, developing personally, becoming a better writer in a second language, completing my studies, teacher training, and teaching full-time.

The first self-published version of my memoir was called "Struggles of Strangers: Of Bonding and Freedom." It was eventually shortlisted for the 2019 Restless Books Prize for New Immigrant Writing in New York. Shortly, I signed a contract with Brandylane Publisher Inc. and Königshausen und Neumann to get a polished version of my memoir with a new title published in the US and in Germany.

Since then, I have presented my memoir at many intercultural events, for instance, at the International Conference on Ethnic and Religious Conflict Resolution and Peacebuilding in New York, but also at smaller local events such as in city libraries in Germany.

Promoting the book is a new challenge that encourages me to leave my comfort zone and try new ways to connect with people. Social media is big here. Let me come back to why I do all this. What are the key messages of my memoir? If I had to break it down into three, it would be: 1. Act with courage and willpower 2. Act with openness and love, and 3. Act here and now for yourself and others.

Junis Sultan studied in Frankfurt am Main, Eichstätt and at California State University Fullerton. He received a Fulbright and a Horizonte Scholarship. For six years, he has taught English, politics, and economics as a high school teacher in Frankfurt am Main. He is pursuing a doctorate in Modern Political Theory at the University of Heidelberg.

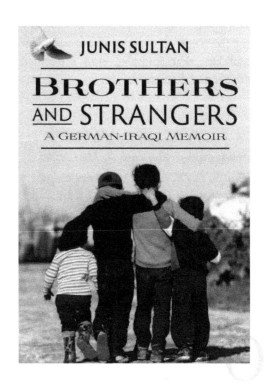

Cliff Hangers
by Jenna Greene

There is a reason some series are ultra-successful while others fall flat. Some of it has to do with the protagonist or villain not catching the reader's heart, while others have to do with the writing style or the characters' obstacles. But in terms of the investment of the reader, a lot of the time, it comes down to the structure.

For many people, investing in a novel is an investment of time, energy, and emotion. Readers go on a journey with highs and lows, impacting how they view the world. Many people adore reading and will gobble up anything anytime for any price. Others enjoy it but struggle to find the time to commit to the activity. At the end of a book, the readers want to feel like they went somewhere and that their energy was well spent.

This is why readers often feel a bit ripped off when they come to the end of a book and find no resolution to the plot or characters and are led to a cliffhanger that insists they read the next novel in the series. It feels like a money grab or a waste of time. They might purchase the next book, but chances are ... they won't.

So how do some series avoid this feeling in their readers? How do they keep the reader interested in a longer tale without offending their audience?

Jenna Greene is a YA/ Children's author from Alberta, Canada. She is also an elementary school teacher. When she isn't reading or writing, she enjoys dance and dragon boat racing. Jenna is known for her Reborn Marks series, her Imagine series, and her picture books.

Structure each book with a problem that is resolved. That way, the reader feels like the book accomplished something. They feel satisfied at the end of the novel. To keep them interested in the series or wanting more, that has to do with an over-arching theme that can be developed – but doesn't have to be. Destroy the death star, but leave the empire in existence. Survive the Hunger Games... but the games still exist, as does President Snow and the Capital.

Wrap up the novel's conflict, leaving a thread of a larger conflict to be tackled in the next.

The Left Turn: Two Lives Worlds Apart by Becky Parker Geist

How did you get your book published?

I'm the founder and CEO of Pro Audio Voices Inc, providing audiobook production, distribution and marketing. The company published my novel, though most of the process was up to me as an indie author. Pro Audio Voices offers AMPlify, the only direct sale platform for audiobooks, giving authors the highest royalties and most control while also delivering great support like the Etsy of audiobooks. The timing was perfect for doing an audio-first launch, which until now was almost impossible for indie authors. Publishing The Left Turn also gave me a way to experience our own marketing and distribution programs as an author.

What do you like to do when you're not writing?

I am passionate about the work we do at Pro Audio Voices, so mostly, I like to be doing that—inspiring the world and empowering authors. The AMPlify launch has been my focus for months. It's a game-changer for authors and listeners. I also love working on the full-cast projects we do. I bring all my theatre production experience to that work; it is energizing and fun. We do a full range of production, from single narrators to full cast. I like to be with family, be outside, bike, and play games for downtime.

What was one of the most surprising things you learned in creating your book?

How great it can be to work with a skilled editor. Though many years ago, I published a few titles; it was before I really knew much about the publishing process. With this novel, it was the first time I had a full grasp of what to do, and also my first experience working with an editor. It was exhilarating! I love collaboration, and that's what it felt like. I stayed open to learning everything I could, and that made it really fun. Part of what made it great was that David would usually explain why he recommended changes.

As a child, what did you want to do growing up?

I wanted to be a mom, an author, a teacher, and an actor. I've been able to do all those. I started writing books as a 5-year-old and wrote my first chapter book in third grade. I've written poetry, plays, a film script, short stories, nonfiction, kids' books, and this first novel. Little of that got as far as publication, but it all got me closer to where I am now. My life feels like a testament to the fact that holding an intention leads to manifestation. Things I consistently have as what I desire and believe show up.

Soulworm by Edward Willett

When did you first realize you wanted to be a writer?

Like most writers, I started as a voracious reader, and from a very early age, I was enamoured with science fiction and fantasy. I wrote my first short story when I was 11 years old: "Kastra Glazz, Hypership Test Pilot," and I was hooked. I wrote constantly, including three full novels in high school, which I shared with my classmates, discovering I could write stories people enjoyed. Toward the end of high school, I decided I wanted to be a professional writer. I started with a journalism degree (reasoning that nobody could make a living as a writer right off the bat—especially not back in those pre-Internet, pre-Amazon, pre-effective-self-publishing days) and worked for several years as a newspaper reporter and editor, and then as the communications officer for a science centre, before quitting my job and becoming a full-time freelancer. My thirtieth anniversary as a full-time writer is this fall.

How do you schedule your life when you're writing?

Every day I have a plethora of projects in various states of completion, not just writing ones but also editing and publishing ones. I prioritize based on what's due next. Typically, if I'm writing a novel, I try to get in a couple of sessions of a couple of hours, morning and afternoon. Since I'm a pretty fast writer, that can get me through the first draft of a novel within a month.

What would you say is your interesting writing quirk?

I hate writing in my nice quiet home office. I write much better in a coffee shop or pub. The white noise of a crowded space doesn't bother me when I'm writing, although if people sit too close to me and have detailed conversations that I can overhear, I have to put on headphones and listen to music.

Is there anything you would like to confess about as an author?

People tell me I'm prolific, but in fact, I'm a terrible procrastinator. I could have written twice as many books as I have if not for a streak of laziness. At least, that's how it feels to me!

As a child, what did you want to do when you grew up?

Until I settled on writing, I wanted to be a scientist, and I maintain an interest in science (originally piqued by reading science fiction); I wrote a weekly science column for newspapers and radio for many years and have written several books on science and engineering, so although I'm not a scientist, I've maintained a connection to science!

The Eloquence of Effort: Beware the Path of Least Resistance by Indar Maharaj

When did you first realize you wanted to be a writer?

I never aspired to be a professional writer. However, following my official retirement, I adopted writing as a creative alternative instead of recklessly wasting time in aimless pursuits.

How do you schedule your life when you're writing?

Though I strive to meet daily objectives, I have no rigorous schedule. Besides the times assigned to trivial rounds, all other times are spent reading and/or writing.

What would you say is your most interesting writing quirk?

Just before thrashing my sorry behind, my dad would scream: the easiest way to succeed is to work hard. A life lesson that has guided my writing routine and has compelled me to face difficult tasks courageously.

How did you get your book published?

A tedious journey with endless rejections, personal insults and myriad encounters with literary sharks. To conserve meager resources, I decided to self-publish.

Where did you get your information or idea for your book?

The theme crystallized in my mind after reading Jeremy Rifkin's book Entropy. Unlike Rifkin, instead of focusing on environmental aspects, I opted to explore the personal benefits of neutralizing the adverse effects of this law on the human organism.

What do you like to do when you're not writing?

Inspired by the work of Gandhi, the messages enshrined in Genesis, the Bhagavad Gita and other religious texts, I try to engage each moment of every day in productive pursuits.

What was one of the most surprising things you learned in creating your book?

The learning derived from the research/writing process has profoundly impacted my way of life. The deeper I plunged into the book's central theme, the more conscious I became of the adversarial impact of Entropy on daily life. To surrender to this force is to accept defeat. I was no longer reveling in an abstruse academic exercise of esoteric equations. It was as palpable as gravity.

Light Come Out of the Closet
by Dr Roger Leslie

Author Interviews

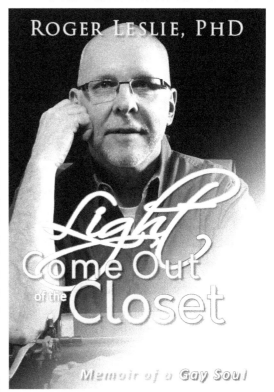

When did you first realize you wanted to be a writer?

The inspiration came to me while sitting in a movie theater. In 1974, my dad took me to see Murder on the Orient Express. That first viewing, I felt giddy with fascination. I kept thinking; I love this movie! As we left the theater, my dad told me my grandmother was a huge Agatha Christie fan and suggested I see the movie again with her. The second time I watched it, my exhilaration about the film's ingenious writing transformed into an epiphany: I want to impact others the way this movie impacts me. At that moment, my destiny solidified. At age 13, I didn't know if I had the talent or fortitude to become an author. However unevolved we are when we're inspired never matters. When we feel to our very soul that something is meant for us, we must only take action and follow where the spirit leads. Life will take us where we're meant to go. The following week I wrote my first short story. I've been writing ever since.

How do you schedule your life when you're writing?

Whether I'm teaching writing workshops (From Inspiration to Publication) or inspirational seminars (FLY–First Last Year), I remind my followers to prioritize. Because I consider my writing the most important contribution I make to the world, I always write first. Over the years, I have had to train myself to focus. It's very easy to glance at my list of emails and think I can get some of those answered and THEN write. I've done that before, but it dilutes my concentration and demands that I shift mental gears from what I did first and revise for the writing to give it my best. Doing what matters most FIRST ensures that you have a great day. Once you've done what you care about most, everything else is just extra that makes your life feel fuller and more diverse.

What would you say is your interesting writing quirk?

I've been in the publishing industry for five decades.
I've worn many hats: author, publisher, editor, writing coach, Booklist reviewer, writing teacher and professor. Working with so many people in these diverse roles taught me that nothing is really a quirk. Whatever works to spark creativity is a blessing, not an oddity. Having said that, however, I will share that I always meditate before writing. My focus is always to clear my subconscious mind to get it out of the way so creative ideas can emerge from my subconscious to create something riveting. From that same perspective, I have learned to do as little preplanning of any book as possible. When I'm inspired to write a book—fiction or nonfiction—I nurture the idea that excites me enough to move to the computer and start writing that first page. From there, I keep opening, opening, opening my mind to see where that first draft leads. Some of my best writing has come while flying blind and watching what my subconscious revealed to conscious-level me as I wrote.

So for anyone who is an author or aspires to be one, I encourage you to trust your process, no matter how "quirky" someone else might see. Do what feels natural to you, and you will find a process that makes your creativity thrive.

The Proximity of Stars by Benedict Stuart

When did you first realize you wanted to be a writer?

Funnily enough, when I was a kid, my dream was to be a writer. Maybe I had no idea then what that actually meant. By all means, being a writer is hard work. There are no shortcuts or 'hacks'.

Working smart is not exactly applicable here, unfortunately. The reader will always sense that. However, the work is rewarding in many ways, not only financially.

After all, the writer leaves something behind, gets to know various people, discusses different topics of interest, freely expresses personal opinions etc.

How did you get your book published?

It was not easy, to be honest, but I am glad Next Chapter approved my manuscript after careful consideration.

Perhaps it is appropriate to say that this young and promising publishing company deserves praise.

It is truly international, people-oriented and gives a chance to independent authors from all walks of life.

The business model the company has created is really innovative and modern.

The community itself is remarkable.

Where did you get your information or idea for your book?

Maybe it sounds a bit banal, but real life is, in fact, a very good source of ideas and inspiration.

In other words, one's own experience could be a valuable contribution. We sometimes underestimate our uniqueness, including our life circumstances, personal growth and the precious lessons we learn daily. Thus sharing our thoughts, feelings, and understanding is enriching. Especially via modern technology, allowing for worldwide coverage.

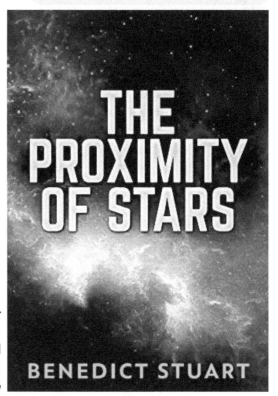

What do you like to do when you're not writing?

That is a good question. I guess most writers should have their day jobs - be sociable, active, communicative and above all, inspiring other people. Allegedly, with a good sense of humor as well.

As a child, what did you want to do when you grew up?

As I said, I wanted to be a writer, but then again, I did not mean I would have only one job in the future. People nowadays must be flexible, versatile, and adaptable, keeping up with the latest developments in any professional area or pastime. 'As the saying goes, everyone has a book inside them.'

Killer With Ice Eyes by J L Hill

When did you first realize you wanted to be a writer?

I knew early in life that I was going to be a writer. My friends and I traced comic characters (Marvels), and I would write what I thought would be the next story.

How do you schedule your life when you're writing?

I usually do my best writing late at night. I am starting around midnight and going for three or four hours.

What would you say is your interesting writing quirk?

I do most of my writing on my computer, but when I come to parts that are really intense for one reason or another, I write long hand because it is faster that way. I can give my ideas down quicker than I could type them.

Where did you get your information or idea for your book?

Ideas come from multiple places depending on the genre I am writing. For example, I'll get ideas for sci-fi from news stories about discoveries or some political stance on a problem. Also, I'll get ideas for a crime novel from people I know or someone I see while people-watching. I got a big chunk of a story from a guy's name; he became the perfect government agent.

How do you process and deal with negative book reviews?

I don't let them bother me. If the review says true, I file it away in the back of my mind for future writing. If the review seems to miss the book's point or the reviewer doesn't like the type of story I wrote, you can't please everyone. Sometimes, negative reviews tell me I hit the bullseye; they don't like the story for what I wanted it to say, which means others will enjoy it for those reasons.

Soap-Stud & Blue-Movie Girl by David Godolphin

When did you first realize you wanted to be a writer?

I woke up one day when I was 18, knowing I wanted to write novels.

What would you say is your interesting writing quirk?

Writing comedy, I like to address the "Dear Reader". Jane Austen did it, and Ian Richardson and Kevin Spacey (both brilliantly) talked to the viewer in the UK/ US versions of House of Cards.

Where did you get your information or idea for your book?

I've loved Hollywood novels ever since I read Harold Robbins' The Carpetbaggers (1961) – still unsurpassed for sheer readability. A friend in Sussex whose sister married screen star James Mason urged me to write a Hollywood book.

What was one of the most surprising things you learned in creating your book?

It is easy to reshape an incident from your life into a character's different background.

How do you process and deal with negative book reviews?

Is it criticism you can learn from, or did they miss the point? I have worked in London and the Persian Gulf and travelled extensively in Canada and the USA. Under the pen name of David Gee, I have published four previous novels, most recently the Mafia romance Lillian and the Italians, in which a Sicilian Prince helps an English widow come to terms with having a gay son. I lived on the Sussex coast near Brighton; he is in year two of a Parkinson's diagnosis. A sequel to Soap-Stud & Blue-Movie Girl is due next year, and I am writing a follow-on to Lillian, set in Spain. My website is https://www.davidgeebooks.com/

MY LIFE AS AN AUTHOR
J. J. Fauser

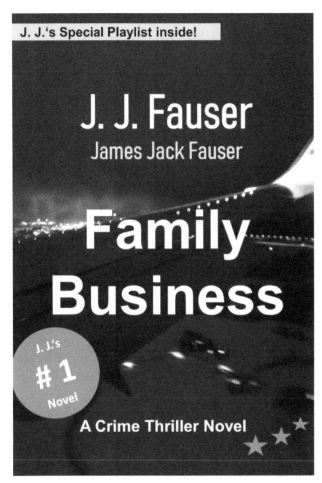

Let me tell you something: I could be a nicer person at work. I can lie and cheat, be brutal and even deadly. The reason is that I'm in the cleaning business. My speciality is the disposal of very nasty characters. Take "Prince Pimp", for example. He imports "fresh meat" from Russia, Belarus, Moldova and poor E.U. countries like Bulgaria and Romania. The poor girls are promised careers in the movies or at least as nannies in German or Swiss households. They fall into these traps like flies, desperate to flee their places of origin without perspective. And the dream of becoming a star in the West, or at least getting a decent job and living, always remains.

Words of Wisdom

After working for a Ministry of State, the EUSAOCT, the Secret Agency for Fighting Organized Crime and Terrorism, recruited J. J. Fauser. Officially, he is a consultant with an international firm. Growing up in a German village, J. J. came to live in England as a teenager and later in the U.S. Since their youth, he got trained in Tae Kwon Do and MMA. He served in a Special Paratrooper Unit and went for training with the FBI in thirty countries J. J. had field operations until now, and he lives in the U.K., the U.S. and Germany. Between missions, he writes.

Prince Pimp is the nickname of Klaus Hefele, whose official royal title as Prince of Saxony-Bamberg was given to him by adoption after a cash payment of two million Euros.

Today he runs a multimillion-dollar enterprise with units all over the world. Prostitution is profitable, but it is only the tip of the iceberg. A very important part of his business is human trafficking, especially of young and desperate girls from Eastern Europe, Latin America and Asia, and money laundering on a very large scale.

Apart from that, Prince Pimp stays clean from drugs and weapons. Not because he has any moral doubts but because he considered the risk of being caught by law enforcement too high. He has always been able to keep himself clean from the evidence of illegal affairs until now.

Until now means I'm on to him, and I will take him down royally, period. You'll know about it too because I will write my next book about it. "Cold Blood and Money" will be the title.

NO LIMITS!
PD Alleva

I write books, that's what I do. Good ones, crazy ones, fun books, entertaining books, scary creepy books that are absolutely insane, books with depth and books with excitement, and books that rip out the heart of humanity and throws it on a slab to be feasted on. Yeah, that's what I do, I write books. Any questions?

There are no limits to the imagination other than what we place on ourselves. Stephen King taught me this most valuable lesson. As did Ray Bradbury, Clive Barker, James Herbert, and Pulp Fiction magazines.

Growing up, I was always intrigued by how far an author could go in a story. How they stretched the limits and just let it all hang out. This is an important part of a writer's life, especially a writer indulging in horror, dark fantasy, and sci-fi novels. I often sat back after writing a gruesome or psychologically scathing scene and asked myself if it was too over the top or if the scene pushed some invisible boundary, and I wasn't sure if I should cross that boundary. However, I wouldn't say I like limits and refuse to write around what could be deemed as societal norms, limits, or boundaries.

When I sat down to write my horror fantasy novel, Jigglyspot and the Zero Intellect, this was the most important aspect I had on my mind. My goal with Jigglyspot was to metaphorically cut my skull open, release every bit of imagination I could discover, and allow it to spill all over the page. Between birthing demonic spiders, entering hell and damnation through the subconscious, and some strange, albeit mind-numbing inner ear problems, the story features a wtf moment in just about every chapter. And it was all done by design, said design being: let it all out.

So, the point of this article is, don't limit yourself. If you're writing a novel, do yourself a favor and refuse to adhere to limits. Don't pull punches. If you've got something to say, write it down and let it loose. Allow your imagination to soar to new heights that you could never imagine.

But don't take my word for it. Read Jigglyspot and discover just how far the imagination can go.

Keep reading.

TEEN MOTHERING: A CHALLENGING BUT DOABLE SITUATION

Michelle Swann

DR. MICHELLE SWANN

Dr. Michelle Swann has worked at universities in Switzerland and Canada. Her recent book, Teenaged Mothers: Designing a Fabulous Life is close to her heart as she was a teen mom. Dr. Michelle Swann's Ph.D. looked at how the most expensive schools in the world marketed themselves historically and how the Swiss Tourism Agency marketed Switzerland as a country of natural-born educators to support their private school-based tourism business. She has taught teachers in training the history of education, schooling, and childhood. She has also taught classes in popular culture and international relations. In her spare time, she sails, rows, and hikes.

Teen motherhood is a big issue in the United States, Canada, and worldwide. Statistics show that less than 2% of teenage mothers ever get a college degree. According to Statistics Canada, there are more than 17 000 teen mothers in Canada each year. More than 50% of teen moms drop out of high school. In the US, there are over 750 000 teen pregnancies a year. The statistics are daunting. That is why I wrote the book Teen Mothers: Designing a Fabulous Life. I wanted to inspire teen mothers to be excellent mothers, have successful careers, and beat the statistics. I am a teen mom in the less than 2% category as I obtained my doctoral degree, so I know firsthand what it is like to be a teen mother, to live in poverty, and the fight hard to get ahead.

In the book, I advocate tenacity and goal setting. Teen Moms must become instant adults and immediately take full responsibility for themselves and their children. They don't have the luxury of growing up slowly. They need a hard work ethic, staying power, and a future-oriented perspective. They have to set short-term and long-term goals, and most of all, they need to stay in school and get some training which will help land them a well-paying job with good benefits that they will need to support their family properly. This is why there is a heavy focus in the book on the career planning process and financial planning.

Teen moms need more than career planning and financial advice. They also need practical information about pregnancy, childbirth, baby care, and parenting. The book gives them this information as well. The book also deals with touchy subjects, like telling your parents you are pregnant and ensuring you are always treated respectfully. Teen moms must demand respect from people and push away those who don't respect their choice to keep their children. They must stand up for themselves and speak out, which is not always easy when you are younger.

The Multitude of Personalities Made Simple

by A.A. Hadi White

Reviewer: Nicholus Schroeder

"

I used to be like everyone else: eat, sleep and 'do what you got to do'. Until my life turned upside down, and I found myself in a position where learning about human personalities and behavior, psychology and deception is a must to keep myself safe. The "Lost Between Details" project started in 2016.

A.A. Hadi White

The Multitude of Personality Made Simple is an educational self-help book by A. A. Hadi White.

It touches on the human psyche and aims to explain, in simple terms, how our personality influences the things we do. At the heart of this book is a discussion of personality types and how they're not as basic as you may believe. The intricacies of the human soul are explored in depth throughout each chapter, and examples of the current subject are provided to help with comprehension.

The referenced material is taken from historical events to give you a better understanding of the personality in question.

This is a book that not only aims to help you understand human nature but also gets you in tune with yourself Stimulating is a word that best describes my experience reading *The Multitude of Personality Made Simple'*.

A. A. Hadi White did a fantastic job at breaking down his ideas into small chunks that I could approach individually. This helped me to grasp his concepts and understand his expressive train of thought. His explanations were brief and to the point while still providing enough detail to make sense. Each example not only helped to further solidify the point raised but also made it fun when engaging with the stories starring notable figures from the past. The author balances enlightenment and entertainment so well that I read the entire book in one sitting without feeling fatigued or bored. This is an interesting book that is both educational and a joy to consume.

Deadly Waters: The Vietnam Naval War And Its Aftermath

by Randy Miller

Reviewer: Jeyran Main

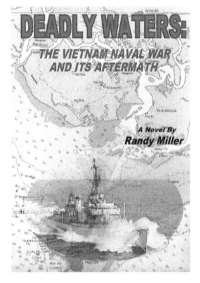

> *This is a book on love, friendship, devotion to duty, the history of a nation and the aftermath of war. It is keenly written and skilfully presented. An enlightening book that inspires thought for every fan of historical books that reflect on war and its after-effects.*
>
> EmunahAn

D*eadly Waters* is a historical fiction about Zack Martin enlisting in the Navy for the United States.

His simple life is set aside, and he says goodbye to his girlfriend. Zack is a young man from a rural part of Vermont.

As a naval destroyer, he is introduced to many things but also learns a lot. However, what he witnesses and endures carries on with him when he returns home. What transpires in this book is very relatable to those who have been in the army or enjoy reading about the Vietnam War. It touches on many subject matters that are precise and real, even though it is a fictional tale. For instance, the depictions of military rivalries and rank structures were truthfully told.

Many mental issues always carry forward with those who have encountered warfare. Important matters such as PTSD and relative mental terms are discussed in this book.

The brotherly bond with his shipmates and the connection between the characters was also heartfelt. You instantly bond with the protagonist and constantly consider ensuring all is well.

What should be remembered is how the story is based on true historical facts.

The descriptive writing allows the reader to visualize what the sailors had to face in the surreal land. This increases the pleasure of reading the story and informs the reader of the reality.

Those who dedicate their life this way truly leave their loved ones and their normal lives to devote themselves to duty and honor.

The progression and intensity of the work are admirable and enjoyable to read. I recommend this book to those who enjoy reading books with such a premise.

Defining Moments of a Free Man from a Black Stream

by Dr Frank L Douglas

Reviewer: Jeyran Main

> Douglas' life story is full of ups and downs. He grows up without knowing his real father and has to work extremely hard to secure a scholarship. Life in the U.S. is not everything that he had dreamed of. This does not stop him from pursuing his dreams and serving his community.
>
> EmunahAn

Defining Moments of a Free Man from a Black Stream is a memoir about Dr Douglas being raised in Guyana, how he comes from a low-income family living in struggling conditions, and the challenges he faces growing up.

His scholarship and attending university opens doors to much more opportunities and endeavours; however, he experiences racism and understands what it means to be of a different race.

The experience does not bring Frank down as his strong personality and demeanour enable him to continue life and fight for what he believes in. With much ambition and many goals, Franks teaches us to overcome mistreatment.

The author also discusses his scientific endeavours. A substantial amount of pages are given about the matter, highlighting projects and passion towards the subject matter.

The work is inspiring and eye-opening for those who do not know, in detail, how racism affects individuals. It explores the issues minorities face in society.

I predominately enjoyed how it approaches racial discrimination in educational institutions and business organizations.

The hope of getting there despite everything is embodied within the book. This emotion truly inspires you and gives you the power to understand that no matter what, you can always overcome and succeed.

While recommending this book, it is appropriate for those who like to read memoirs and enjoy encouraging reads.

I Will Make of Thee a Great Nation: Old Testament Stories

by Val D. Greenwood

Reviewer: Jeyran Main

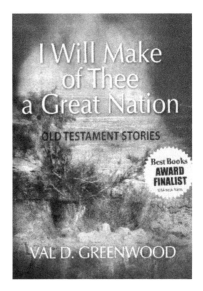

"

I recommend this book to Christians who are struggling with reading the Old Testament of the Bible. This is because most people find it easier to read the New Testament than the Old Testament.

Oyedeji Okikioluwa

Will Make of Thee a Great Nation is a religiously inclined book and a compilation of the Old Testament is taken from the Bible but presented much more simply. The stories are written in such a way as to enable the reader to enjoy every page. With 219 stories displayed chronologically, you are introduced to everything you need to know historically about Christ and the Jewish people of the time. It is an educational read and, above all, made enjoyable for those who wish to embark on a journey receiving enlightenment.

The book contains stories of Abraham and Isaac; David and Goliath; Cain and Abel; Job, and many more. Much attention is given to creating this work, and it is apparent that the author has cared enough to ensure that all is in good standing order.

The footnotes, references, maps, index, pronunciation guide and the added subject index all prove how much work has gone into making this book. Attention to detail has been given to the work.

The cover created for the book is also well thought out and reflects the rich content inside.

The author's hard work pays off when you read all the book's passages. Understanding each story is the aim of the game, and here you truly do get to see what transpires as part of the script.

I recommend this book to anyone who wants to use it as a study guide for their bible studies or wishes to know more about Christianity.

House of Eire: A Hillary Broome Novel

by June Gillam

Reviewer: Jeyran Main

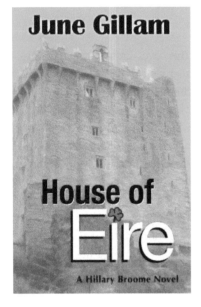

> No matter how far we run from our past, it always has a way of catching up with us. To embrace our future, we need to accept our past with grace, humility, and pride.

Kajori Sheryl Paul

House of Eire is a paranormal murder mystery story. It is the third book of its series and follows Hillary Broome and her husband, Ed, on their honeymoon. It has been a while since they have been married, but nevertheless, they are on their honeymoon and are spending a lovely time in Ireland with their daughter, Claire.

Hillary also meets with her friend Bridget and has much catching up to do. While everything seems to be going exactly as it should, murder, mystery and mayhem happen.

The intense descriptive scenes, constant change of pace, and discussions between the characters keep you intrigued, wanting to know what will happen next. The guessing game is always on the go, and as the author plays with your mind, she also manages to bring a delightful story to the game.

While you wander through the beautiful nature and country, you also get to create memorable moments in your mind of the thrilling nature that the story constructs.

The notion of family and love for one another, no matter the circumstances, was also an additional bonus within the story. Ed was a very supportive husband and was always in pursuit of helping his family.

As you read along, you also notice the attention to detail given to the moments and the story. It is carefully crafted and well thought out.

I recommend this book to those who like to read murder mystery stories and thriller-natured concepts.

Editor's Pick

ERIC THE EARTHWORM BY CHERYL BOND-NELMS

Eric the Earthworm combines beautiful illustrations with a tale that will give every child an uplifting and positive outlook on life. As you turn each page, your eyes are immersed in a world of vibrant color that will make you and your little one smile. A local park resident, Eric becomes jealous of the seemingly more impressive residents who possess a different range of skills and abilities. With a little help and love from Mom, Eric realizes his own greatness and what makes him special and unique.

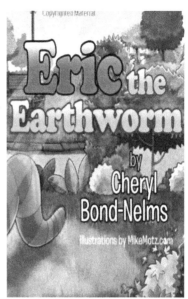

SURVIVING THE BUSINESS OF HEALTHCARE: KNOWLEDGE IS POWER BY BARBARA GALUTIA REGIS M S PA-C

In Surviving the "Business" of Healthcare--Knowledge Is Power!, author Barbara Galutia Regis, MS, PA-C, shares a uniquely useful perspective with readers facing chronic illness and those caring for ill loved ones. Regis has been a healthcare provider, and patient advocate for years and now faces her own challenge of a lifetime: a cancer diagnosis. Writing from both sides of the healthcare system, Regis addresses many concerns faced by all of us when we address our health; readers may open Surviving the "Business" of Healthcare--Knowledge Is Power! to any page and find a topic that sparks conversation.

FEAR NOT, DREAM BIG, & EXECUTE: TOOLS TO SPARK YOUR DREAM AND IGNITE YOUR FOLLOW-THROUGH BY JEFF MEYER

Packed with life lessons and tools, Jeff Meyer invites you to linger where you will. More like a weekly dose of encouragement than a novel, you can pick and choose the lessons that hit home. Sit with them until they stick.
As they shout at Camp Randall in Madison, WI, where Jeff resides with his wife Amy, "Jump Around." Cue music...
Overcome the self-inflicting wounds that have kept you from pursuing your dream.
Break free from others' expectations & discover YOUR dream.
Engage your own entrepreneurship mojo. Efficiently execute using very practical productivity strategies.

CPSIA information can be obtained
at www.ICGtesting.com
Printed in the USA
BVHW021158140723
667244BV00011B/751

9 781988 680323